> ♪ **UMT Tip:** Before beginning your exam, write out the Circle of Fifths. Write the order of flats and sharps. Write the Major keys on the outside of the circle and the relative minor keys on the inside of the circle.

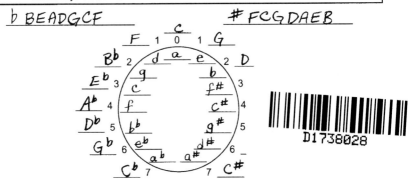

> ♪ **UMT Tip:** Intervals can be inverted by moving the upper (top) note down an octave or by moving the lower (bottom) note up an octave.

1. a) Write the following harmonic intervals below each of the given notes. Use whole notes.

diminished 2   minor 7   Augmented 5   Major 6   Perfect 8

b) Invert the above harmonic intervals in the given clef. Name the inversions.

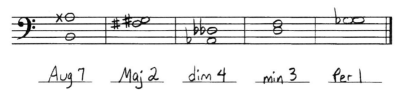

Aug 7   Maj 2   dim 4   min 3   Per 1

ULTIMATE MUSIC THEORY
INTERMEDIATE EXAM SET #1 - EXAM #1

♪ **UMT Tip:** The Dominant triad of a minor key contains the raised 7th (Leading Note).

2. a) Write the following solid triads in close position in the Treble Clef. Use the correct Key Signature and any necessary accidentals. Use whole notes.

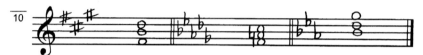

Supertonic triad of
A Major
in second inversion

Dominant triad of
b flat minor harmonic
in root position

Mediant triad of
E flat Major
in first inversion

b) Write the following solid triads in close position in the Bass Clef. Use accidentals. Use whole notes.

Subdominant triad of
g sharp minor harmonic
in first inversion

Dominant triad of
c minor harmonic
in second inversion

Submediant triad of
E Major
in root position

♪ **UMT Tip:** The quality/type of a triad is whether the triad is Major or minor. The quality/type is based on the Major scale of the root note.

c) Identify the root note and the quality/type of each of the following open position triads.

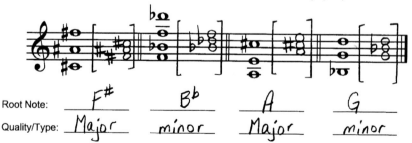

Root Note: __F#__ __Bb__ __A__ __G__

Quality/Type: __Major__ __minor__ __Major__ __minor__

♪ **UMT Tip:** Draw a staff in the margin. Write the interval above the Tonic note of the given melody. The top note names the new key.

3. The following melody is in the key of D flat Major.
   a) Transpose the given melody UP an Augmented third. Use the correct Key Signature.
   b) Name the key of the new melody.

Key: D flat Major

Key: __F# Major__

♪ **UMT Tip:** Name the accidentals in order of the Key Signature. When accidentals are in the correct Key Signature order, the key is usually Major.

The following melody has been written using accidentals instead of a Key Signature.
   c) Name the key of the given melody.
   d) Rewrite the given melody using the correct Key Signature and any necessary accidentals.

Key: __F# minor__   Sharps F# C# G# (E#)
                                        Raised 7th

♪ **UMT Tip:** Scales may be written with or without a center bar line after the highest note. Either way is correct.

4. Write the following scales, ascending and descending, using the correct Key Signature and any necessary accidentals for each. Use whole notes.

10 a) f sharp minor natural scale in the Treble Clef.

b) C sharp Major scale in the Bass Clef.

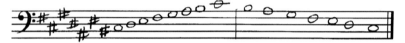

c) relative minor scale, harmonic form, of D flat Major in the Bass Clef. (b♭ min. harm.)

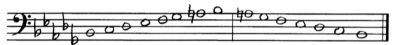

d) Tonic Major scale of f sharp minor in the Treble Clef. (F♯ Major)

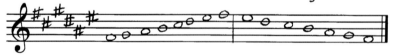

e) Enharmonic Tonic minor scale, melodic form, of e flat minor in the Bass Clef. (d♯ min. mel.)

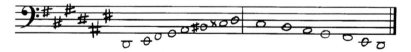

> ♪ **UMT Tip:** The final note in the Bass Clef can be either the Tonic or Dominant note of the Major or relative minor key.

5. For each of the following cadences, name:
    a) the key.
    b) the type of cadence (Perfect, Plagal or Imperfect).

10

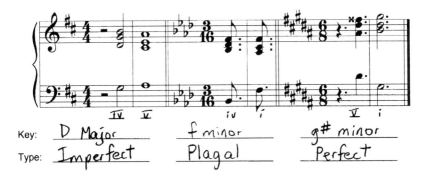

Key: D Major _____ f minor _____ g# minor _____

Type: Imperfect _____ Plagal _____ Perfect _____

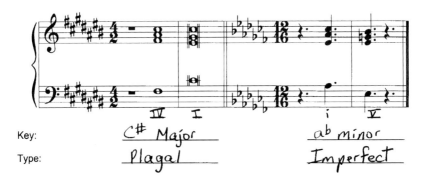

Key: _____ C# Major _____ ab minor _____

Type: _____ Plagal _____ Imperfect _____

♪ **UMT Tip:** A musical excerpt does not always start or end on the Tonic note.

6. For each of the following excerpts:
    a) Name the key.
    b) Add the correct Time Signature below the bracket.

Key: _E Major_

Key: _f minor_

Key: _F Major_

Key: _c# minor_

Key: _G Major_

ULTIMATE MUSIC THEORY
INTERMEDIATE EXAM SET #1 - EXAM #1

> ♪ **UMT Tip:** Write the Basic Beat and the Pulse below each measure. Cross off the Basic Beat as each beat is completed.

7. Add rests below each bracket to complete each measure.

♪ **UMT Tip:** Identify the distances between the notes to find the pattern.

8. a) Name the following scales as blues, chromatic, Major pentatonic, minor pentatonic, octatonic or whole tone.

whole tone

minor pentatonic

Major pentatonic

Blues

chromatic

b) For the following Major Key Signatures, identify the technical degree name of each note.

Mediant   Dominant   Submediant

Leading note   Supertonic

ULTIMATE MUSIC THEORY
INTERMEDIATE EXAM SET #1 - EXAM #1

> ♪ **UMT Tip:** Before looking at the possible definitions, look at the Term and identify the
> definition. Then match the definition with one of the given definitions.

9. Match each musical term with its English definition. (Not all definitions will be used.)

___
10

Term		Definition
spiritoso	_h_	a) slow and solemn
troppo	_C_	b) without
vivace	_K_	c) too much
grave	_a_	d) with
fortepiano	_j_	e) quiet, tranquil
senza	_b_	f) one string; depress the left (piano) pedal
loco	_i_	g) three strings; release the left (piano) pedal
con	_d_	h) spirited
una corda	_f_	i) return to the normal register
tranquillo	_e_	j) loud, then suddenly soft
		k) lively, brisk

> ♪ **UMT Tip:** When identifying the Key Signature, a minor key will usually have an accidental on the raised 7th note - the Leading note.

10. Analyze the following piece of music by answering the questions below.

10

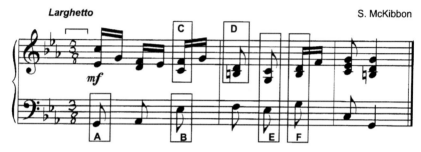

I Don't Want to Go to Bed!

Larghetto

S. McKibbon

a) Name the key of this piece. _C minor_

b) Explain the tempo of this piece. _Larghetto - not as slow as Largo_

c) Add the Time Signature directly on the music.

d) Identify the technical degree name of the note at the letter **A**. _Dominant_

e) Identify the technical degree name of the note at the letter **B**. _Mediant_

f) Name the interval at the letter **C**. _Perfect 4_

g) Name the interval at the letter **D**. _minor 3_

h) For the triad at **E**, name: Root: _C_ Type/Quality: _minor_ Position: _1st inv._

i) For the triad at **F**, name: Root: _G_ Type/Quality: _Major_ Position: _root_

j) Identify the cadence in measure 3 as Perfect, Imperfect or Plagal. _Imperfect_

Total Score: ____
100

> ♪ **UMT Tip:** Before beginning your exam, write out the Circle of Fifths. Write the order of flats and sharps. Write the Major keys on the outside of the circle and the relative minor keys on the inside of the circle.

♭ BEADGCF   # FCGDAEB

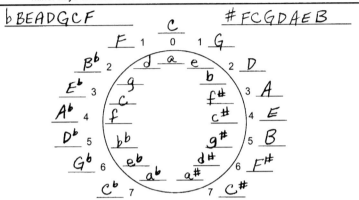

> ♪ **UMT Tip:** Begin by finding the Major or Perfect interval and then adjusting the lower (bottom) note to make the interval minor, diminished or Augmented.

1. a) Write the following harmonic intervals below each of the given notes. Use whole notes.

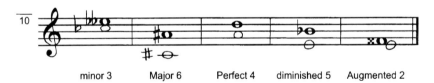

minor 3   Major 6   Perfect 4   diminished 5   Augmented 2

b) Invert the above harmonic intervals in the given clef. Name the inversions.

Maj 6   min 3   Per 5   Aug 4   dim 7

ULTIMATE MUSIC THEORY
INTERMEDIATE EXAM SET #1 - EXAM #2

> ♪ **UMT Tip:** When writing a triad in first inversion or second inversion, first write it in root position in [square brackets] at the end of the measure. Then write the inversion at the beginning of the measure.

2. a) Write the following solid triads in close position in the Treble Clef. Use accidentals. Use whole notes.

Mediant triad of
B flat Major
in second inversion

Dominant triad of
D Major
in root position

Subdominant triad of
g minor harmonic
in first inversion

b) Write the following solid triads in close position in the Bass Clef. Use the correct Key Signature and any necessary accidentals. Use whole notes.

Supertonic triad of
G flat Major
in first inversion

Submediant triad of
f sharp minor harmonic
in second inversion

Subdominant triad of
A flat Major
in root position

> ♪ **UMT Tip:** In open position, one note of the triad may be repeated. Rewrite the triad in root position in [square brackets] at the end of the measure. Use each note only once.

c) Identify the root note and the quality/type of each of the following open position triads.

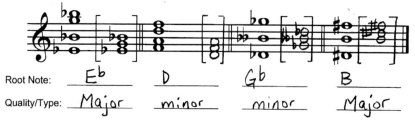

Root Note: ___Eb___ ___D___ ___Gb___ ___B___

Quality/Type: ___Major___ ___minor___ ___minor___ ___Major___

♪ **UMT Tip:** When transposing a melody to a new key, a Major key will ALWAYS remain a Major key.

3. The following melody is in the key of E flat Major.
   a) Transpose the given melody UP an Augmented fourth. Use the correct Key Signature.
   b) Name the key of the new melody.

Key: E flat Major

Key: A Major

♪ **UMT Tip:** Name the accidentals in order of the Key Signature. When accidentals are in the correct Key Signature order, the key is usually Major.

The following melody has been written using accidentals instead of a Key Signature.
   c) Name the key of the given melody.
   d) Rewrite the given melody using the correct Key Signature and any necessary accidentals.

Key: Dᵇ Major   Flats: Bᵇ Eᵇ Aᵇ Dᵇ Gᵇ

ULTIMATE MUSIC THEORY
INTERMEDIATE EXAM SET #1 - EXAM #2

> ♪ **UMT Tip:** Chromatic scale using any standard notation - starts and ends on the same Tonic note and does not use any letter name more than twice. Whole tone scale using any standard notation - starts and ends on the same Tonic note and uses the same notes and accidentals (all sharps or all flats) ascending and descending.

4. Write the following scales, ascending and descending, using accidentals. Use whole notes.

10

a) Chromatic scale beginning on D in the Treble Clef. Use any standard notation.

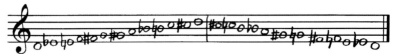

b) Whole tone scale beginning on A flat in the Bass Clef. Use any standard notation.

c) Relative minor scale, harmonic form, of B Major in the Bass Clef. $(g\# min. harm.)$

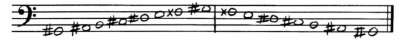

d) Tonic minor scale, natural form, of F Major in the Treble Clef. $(f min. nat.)$

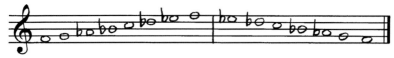

e) Enharmonic Tonic Major scale of C sharp Major in the Bass Clef. $(D^b Major)$

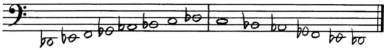

> ♪ **UMT Tip:** Each Key Signature will have two options - the Major key and its relative minor key. Check to see if the final note is the Tonic or the Dominant note in the Major key or in the relative minor key.

5. For each of the following cadences, name:
   a) the key.
   b) the type of cadence (Perfect, Plagal or Imperfect).

Key: <u>a minor</u>   <u>B♭ Major</u>   <u>f# minor</u>
Type: <u>Perfect</u>   <u>Imperfect</u>   <u>Imperfect</u>

Key: <u>G♭ Major</u>   <u>a# minor</u>
Type: <u>Plagal</u>   <u>Imperfect</u>

ULTIMATE MUSIC THEORY
INTERMEDIATE EXAM SET #1 - EXAM #2

> ♪ **UMT Tip:** Look for single notes or groups of 3 notes to determine whether the Time Signature is Simple Time or Compound Time.

6. For each of the following excerpts:
   a) Name the key.
   b) Add the correct Time Signature below the bracket.

10

Key: _eb minor_

Key: _D Major_

Key: _Bb Major_

Key: _g# minor_

Key: _Cb Major_

ULTIMATE MUSIC THEORY
INTERMEDIATE EXAM SET #1 - EXAM #2

> ♪ **UMT Tip:** Write the Basic Beat and pulse below each measure. When indicating to JOIN pulses, use the "+" plus sign. When indicating to NOT join pulses use the "~" tilde sign.

7. Add rests below each bracket to complete each measure.

ULTIMATE MUSIC THEORY
INTERMEDIATE EXAM SET #1 - EXAM #2

♪ **UMT Tip:** Use the Circle of Fifths to identify the Key Signature.

8. a) Name the following notes.

___
10

The Leading note of d minor harmonic is _____C#_____.

The Mediant of G Major is _____B_____.

The Dominant of e minor melodic is _____B_____.

The Supertonic of C# Major is _____D#_____.

The Submediant of b♭ minor melodic (ascending) is _____G_____.

b) For each of the following, name the minor key. Identify the technical degree name of the note.

minor key: _____eb minor_____   _____b minor_____   _____g minor_____

Technical
degree name: _____Supertonic_____   _____Tonic_____   _____Subdominant_____

minor key: _____a# minor_____   _____ab minor_____

Technical
degree name: _____Dominant_____   _____Mediant_____

ULTIMATE MUSIC THEORY
INTERMEDIATE EXAM SET #1 - EXAM #2

♪ **UMT Tip:** Before looking at the possible definitions, look at the Term and identify the definition. Remember that not all definitions will be used.

9. Match each musical term with its English definition. (Not all definitions will be used.)

Term		Definition
ma	_e_	a) becoming quicker
con brio	_k_	b) lightly
accelerando	_a_	c) much, very
bene	_f_	d) always, continuously
leggiero	_b_	e) but
meno mosso	_j_	f) well
molto	_c_	g) expressive, with expression
più mosso	_i_	h) without
sempre	_d_	i) more movement, quicker
espressivo	_g_	j) less movement, slower
		k) with vigor, spirit

> ♪ **UMT Tip:** The Time Signature is written in both the Treble Clef and the Bass Clef.

10. Analyze the following piece of music by answering the questions below.

Broken Cookies

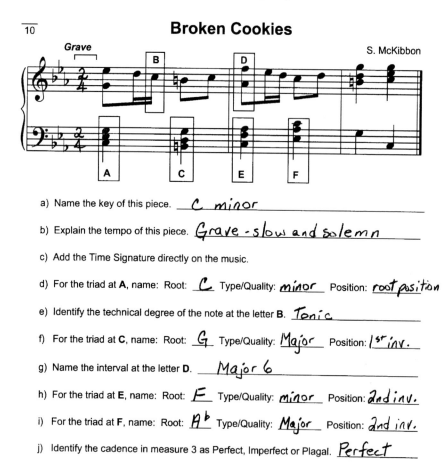

Grave

S. McKibbon

a) Name the key of this piece. _C minor_

b) Explain the tempo of this piece. _Grave - slow and solemn_

c) Add the Time Signature directly on the music.

d) For the triad at **A**, name: Root: _C_ Type/Quality: _minor_ Position: _root position_

e) Identify the technical degree of the note at the letter **B**. _Tonic_

f) For the triad at **C**, name: Root: _G_ Type/Quality: _Major_ Position: _1st inv._

g) Name the interval at the letter **D**. _Major 6_

h) For the triad at **E**, name: Root: _F_ Type/Quality: _minor_ Position: _2nd inv._

i) For the triad at **F**, name: Root: _A♭_ Type/Quality: _Major_ Position: _2nd inv._

j) Identify the cadence in measure 3 as Perfect, Imperfect or Plagal. _Perfect_

1. a) Write the following harmonic intervals below each of the given notes. Use whole notes.

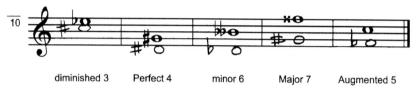

diminished 3   Perfect 4   minor 6   Major 7   Augmented 5

b) Invert the above harmonic intervals in the same clef. Name the inversions. Use whole notes.

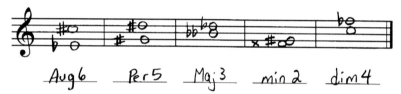

Aug 6   Per 5   Maj 3   min 2   dim 4

c) Write the following melodic intervals above each of the given notes. Use whole notes.

Augmented 2   diminished 5   Major 3   Perfect 8   Major 6

d) Invert the above melodic intervals in the same clef. Name the inversions. Use whole notes.

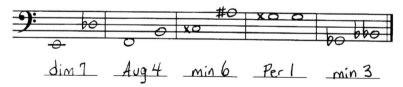

dim 7   Aug 4   min 6   Per 1   min 3

2. Match each description in the left column with the correct solid triad, in close or in open position, in the right column.

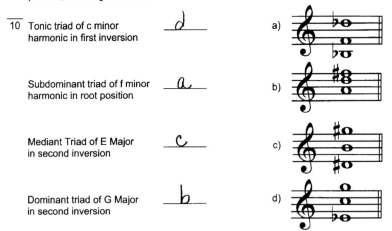

10 Tonic triad of c minor harmonic in first inversion _____d_____

Subdominant triad of f minor harmonic in root position _____a_____

Mediant Triad of E Major in second inversion _____C_____

Dominant triad of G Major in second inversion _____b_____

a)

b)

c)

d)

Write the following triads in close position and solid form. Use a Key Signature and any necessary accidentals. Use whole notes.

e) Supertonic triad of D flat Major in root position

f) Leading note triad of c sharp minor harmonic in first inversion

g) Submediant triad of A Major in second inversion

h) Tonic triad of A flat Major in root position

i) Mediant triad of C sharp Major in second inversion

j) Subdominant triad of c minor harmonic in first inversion

3. The following melody is in the key of A Major.
   a) Transpose the given melody UP a minor third. Use the correct Key Signature. Name the key of the new melody.

   10 b) Transpose the given melody UP a diminished fifth. Use the correct Key Signature. Name the key of the new melody.

Key: A Major

Key: C Major

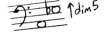

Key: E♭ Major

4. Write the following scales, ascending and descending, in the given clefs. Use whole notes.

10 a) The relative minor scale, melodic form, of C flat Major. Use accidentals. (a♭ min.mel.)

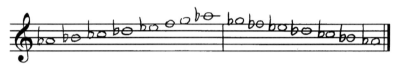

b) The Tonic minor scale, harmonic form, of B Major. Use a Key Signature.

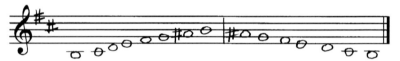

c) G flat Major scale. Use a Key Signature.

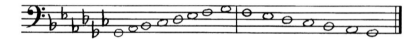

d) Whole Tone scale beginning on F. Use accidentals. Use any standard notation.

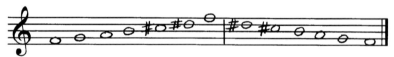

e) Chromatic scale beginning on G. Use accidentals. Use any standard notation.

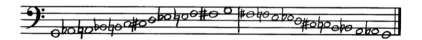

5. For each of the following cadences, name:
   a) the key.
   b) the type of cadence (Perfect, Plagal or Imperfect).

10

I   V   IV   I   iv   i

Key: _A Major_   _G Major_   _ab minor_

Type: _Imperfect_   _Plagal_   _Plagal_

IV   V   V   i

Key: _Gb Major_   _d# minor_

Type: _Imperfect_   _Perfect_

6. For each of the following excerpts:
   a) Name the key.
   b) Add the correct Time Signature below the bracket.

10

Key: *G Major*

Key: *g minor*

Key: *d# minor*

Key: *F Major*

Key: *E Major*

7. Add rests below each bracket to complete each measure.

8. For each of the following:
   a) Name the minor key.
   b) Identify the technical degree name for each note. (Do not use Roman Numerals or abbreviations.)

10

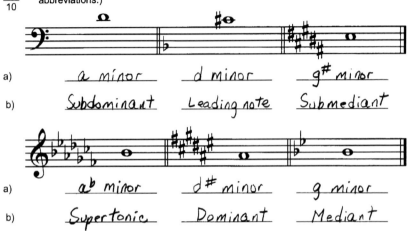

a) *a minor*   *d minor*   *g# minor*

b) Subdominant   Leading note   Submediant

a) *ab minor*   *d# minor*   *g minor*

b) Supertonic   Dominant   Mediant

b) Name the following scales as blues, chromatic, Major pentatonic, minor pentatonic, octatonic or whole tone.

blues

minor pentatonic

Major pentatonic

chromatic

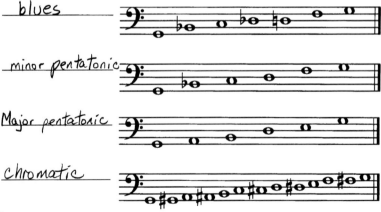

9. For each of the following Italian Terms, circle whether the definition is True or False.

___
10

Term	Definition	True or False		
troppo	too much	(True)	or	False
senza	with	True	or	(False)
sempre	much, very much	True	or	(False)
molto	without	True	or	(False)
non	not	(True)	or	False
meno	less	(True)	or	False
ma	but	(True)	or	False
alla	in the manner of	(True)	or	False
ed	and	(True)	or	False
ben	well	(True)	or	False
colle	little	True	or	(False)

10. Analyze the following piece of music by answering the questions below.

10

Layla's Waltz

S. McKibbon

Allegretto

a) Name the key of this piece. ___G Major___

b) Explain the tempo of this piece. ___Allegretto - fairly fast (not as fast as Allegro)___

c) Add the Time Signature directly on the music.

d) Explain the number at the letter **A**. ___Triplet 3 play 3 in the time of 2 notes of the same value___

e) Identify the cadence in measure 2 as Perfect, Plagal or Imperfect. ___Plagal___

f) Name the intervals at the following letters: **B** ___Per 4___   **c** ___min 6___

g) Identify the cadence in measure 4 as Perfect, Plagal or Imperfect. ___Perfect___

h) Circle a diatonic semitone in this piece. Label it as d.s.

i) How many measures are in this piece? ___Four___

j) Explain the sign at the letter **D**. ___Repeat from the beginning___

1. a) Name the following harmonic intervals.

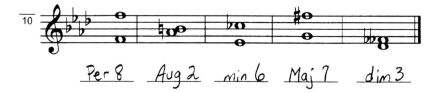

Per 8   Aug 2   min 6   Maj 7   dim 3

b) Invert the above harmonic intervals in the same clef. Name the inversions.

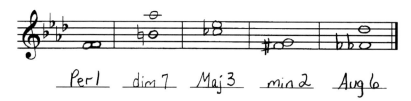

Per 1   dim 7   Maj 3   min 2   Aug 6

c) Name the following melodic intervals.

Aug 1   Maj 3   dim 7   Maj 6   min 2

d) Invert the above melodic intervals in the same clef. Name the inversions.

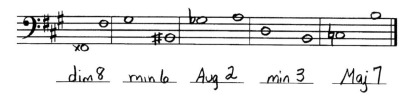

dim 8   min 6   Aug 2   min 3   Maj 7

2. Match each description in the left column with the correct solid triad, in close or in open position, in the right column.

___
10

Subdominant triad of e minor
harmonic in first inversion _____ c _____   a)

Tonic triad of E flat Major
in second inversion _____ g _____   b)

Submediant triad of a sharp minor
harmonic in root position _____ a _____   c)

Mediant triad of D Major
in second inversion _____ b _____   d)

Dominant triad of a minor
harmonic in first inversion _____ h _____   e)

Tonic triad of f minor
harmonic in root position _____ k _____   f)

Subdominant triad of E Major
in second inversion _____ e _____   g)

Supertonic triad of C Major
in root position _____ i _____   h)

Tonic triad of a flat minor
harmonic in first inversion _____ d _____   i)

Dominant triad of d sharp minor
harmonic in root position _____ f _____   j)

Submediant triad of F sharp Major
in second inversion _____ j _____   k)

3. The following melody is in the key of A flat Major.
    a) Transpose the given melody UP a Major second. Use the correct Key Signature.
       Name the key of the new melody.
    b) Transpose the given melody UP an Augmented fifth. Use the correct Key Signature.
       Name the key of the new melody.

10

Key: A flat Major

Key: B♭ Major

Key: E Major

4. Write the following scales, ascending and descending, in the given clefs. Use whole notes.

10 a) The enharmonic relative minor scale, harmonic form, of F sharp Major. Use accidentals. *(e♭ min. harm.)*

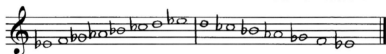

b) The Tonic minor scale, melodic form, of E Major. Use a Key Signature. *(e min. mel.)*

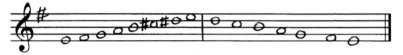

c) A flat Major scale. Use a Key Signature.

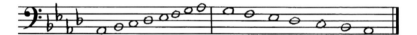

d) Whole Tone scale beginning on B flat. Use accidentals. Use any standard notation.

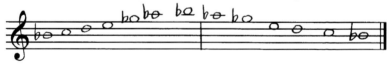

e) Chromatic scale beginning on B. Use accidentals. Use any standard notation.

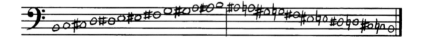

5. For each of the following cadences, name:
   a) the key.
   b) the type of cadence (Perfect, Plagal or Imperfect).

10

IV   I   i'   V   iv   V

Key: __A Major__   __e minor__   __b♭ minor__

Type: __Plagal__   __Imperfect__   __Imperfect__

I   i   IV   V

Key: __e♭ minor__   __F# Major__

Type: __Perfect__   __Imperfect__

6. For each of the following excerpts:
   a) Name the key.
   b) Add the correct Time Signature below the bracket.

10

Key: _C minor_

Key: _A Major_

Key: _e minor_

Key: _Gb Major_

Key: _B Major_

7. Add rests below each bracket to complete each measure.

8. For each of the following:
   a) Name the minor key.
   b) Identify the technical degree name for each note. (Do not use Roman Numerals or abbreviations.)

10

a) _a minor_   _d minor_   _g# minor_

b) _Mediant_   _Supertonic_   _Tonic_

a) _ab minor_   _d# minor_

b) _Dominant_   _Leading note_

c) Name the following notes.

The Submediant of F Major is ___D___.

The Tonic of A flat Major is ___Ab___.

The Subdominant of C sharp Major is ___F#___.

The Leading note of G flat Major is ___F___.

The Supertonic of B flat Major is ___C___.

9. For each of the following Italian Terms, circle whether the definition is True or False.

$\frac{}{10}$

Term	Definition	True or False		
non troppo	not too much	(True)	or	False
con espressione	with vigor, spirit	True	or	(False)
assai	much, very much	(True)	or	False
col	with	(True)	or	False
animato	quiet, tranquil	True	or	(False)
poco	little	(True)	or	False
tre corde	three strings; release the left (piano) pedal	(True)	or	False
una corda	one string; depress the left (piano) pedal	(True)	or	False
grave	graceful	True	or	(False)
senza	without	(True)	or	False
leggiero	softly	True	or	(False)

ULTIMATE MUSIC THEORY
INTERMEDIATE EXAM SET #1 - EXAM #4

10. Analyze the following excerpt by answering the questions below.

<u>10</u>

Ecossaise

Ludwig van Beethoven

Allegro | **A** M.M ♩ = 108 - 120 |

(musical excerpt with markings D >, F, C.S., B, C, E)

a) Name the key of this piece. ___G Major___

b) Explain the tempo of this piece. ___Allegro - fast___

c) Add the Time Signature directly on the music.

d) Explain the term at the letter **A**. ___Maelzel's Metronome: play at a speed of 108-120 quarter notes per minute___

e) Add the correct rest at the letter **B**.

f) For the triad at **C**, name: Root: ___G___ Type/Quality: ___Major___ Position: ___root position___

g) Explain the sign at the letter **D**. ___accent - stressed note___

h) Name the intervals at the following letters: **E** ___dim 5___   **F** ___Maj 2___

i) Circle a chromatic semitone in this piece. Label it as c.s.

j) How many measures are in this excerpt? ___Four___